The Ultimate Truth

The Ultimate Truth

Keith N. Ferreira

iUniverse, Inc.
New York Lincoln Shanghai

The Ultimate Truth

iUniverse books may be ordered through booksellers or by contacting:

iUniverse
2021 Pine Lake Road, Suite 100
Lincoln, NE 68512
www.iuniverse.com
1-800-Authors (1-800-288-4677)

ISBN-13: 978-0-595-35857-1 (pbk)
ISBN-13: 978-0-595-80315-6 (ebk)
ISBN-10: 0-595-35857-8 (pbk)
ISBN-10: 0-595-80315-6 (ebk)

Printed in the United States of America

To My Brother-in-Law,
Horace Assam

Contents

Part One

The Ultimate Truth

The ultimate truth is the law of uncertainty, which states that uncertainty is the only certainty.

Financial Success vs. Saving the World

I would rather save the world any day than be financially successful.

Money vs. Knowledge

Money without knowledge is worthless, while knowledge without money is the basis of culture.

The Middle Class

The middle class can maintain their standards of living by endless innovation and creative entrepreneurship.

Outsourcing of Jobs

Outsourcing of jobs by large corporations is the only way that large corporations can be competitive in the global economy, because of the economies of scale.

So What?

So what if some conspiracy theories are true?

One Wish

In 1972, while I was at the Brooklyn VA Hospital, the Congress granted me one wish. In effect, what they gave me was a blank check, and I told them that I wished for world integration. I have to admit that my relationship with Congress over the years has been a love-hate relationship.

Folks

Folks, the VA has been trying to remove me from the scene for over 30 years, but they haven't succeeded as yet, because there are other members of the government that always get me out of trouble. I don't know who they are, but they always show up when I am having difficulty with the VA. I even believe that some members of the VA get beaten up for mistreating me.

When I Was in the Military

When I was in the military, I was involved in James Bond-type stuff right here in the U.S.

In the Military

In the military, my unofficial rank was SP/4, but my official rank was five star general. I told the military that I wanted to use my unofficial rank. SP/4 is equivalent to a corporal.

Fort Dix

Fort Dix, New Jersey, was known as the home of the Ultimate Weapon. Well, folks, I was, and still am the Ultimate Weapon, and that is why the VA is trying very hard to remove me from the scene. The Congress is only supposed to call on me as a last resort.

I Don't Understand

I don't understand why the U.S. government keeps the American people stupid, while they bring in scientists, technologists, and intellectuals from all over the world.

By the Way Folks

By the way folks, I am also Uncle Sam.

I Would Like to Ask

I would like to ask people who criticize President Bush for his Iraq policy, "Haven't they ever ended up doing the right thing for the wrong reasons?"

People Who Want

People who want to get to the intellectual mountaintop are going to get beaten up by superstitions and disinformation.

Pass Glory

Pass glory can save no one from present and future realities.

Woe Betide (For Mr. Pindar)

Woe betide the person or persons who does not do my homework.

Class

Class dismissed.

Cock Robin

"Who killed Cock Robin?" I killed Cock Robin.

The First Mind Reading Implant

The first mind reading implant was placed in me at the Brooklyn VA Hospital in 1972, and the second was placed in the director of the project who was a black, female scientist. I think that she had hers removed soon after, but mine is still implanted. I am the one who informed the government of this technology. People usually do not hear about the black scientists in the U.S. government, but there are many important black scientists in the U.S. government who are involved in top secret projects. Folks, there are a lot of black mad scientists also who are carrying out diabolical experiments for the U.S. government.

The Concept

I am the one who developed the concept for the Stanford Linear Accelerator.

I Am the One

I am the one who developed the concept of putting Van de Graaff generators in vacuums in order to increase the voltage of the Van de Graaff generators to a billion volts or more.

Charging Capacitors

I am the one who developed the concept of charging capacitors and connecting them in series electromechanically in order to achieve voltages of a billion volts or more.

Digital Cameras

I am the one who developed the concept that is used in digital cameras, digital telescopes, and digital microscopes.

Many Other Concepts

I am the one who developed the concepts for many other developments as well.

When a Cow

When a cow takes a shit, it continues to do what it was doing before. It is as though the cow is thinking, "I can't be bothered with that shit."

I See Nothing Wrong

I see nothing wrong with teaching the theory of creation along with the theory of evolution in public schools. Having alternative views in educational settings is always a good idea. At least, children would have something to discuss and argue about outside of the classroom, instead of eating junk food, drinking sodas, and bullshitting. In elementary, high school, and even college, I was forever arguing about religion and science even though I was not supposed to do so.

The American Eagle

By the way folks, I am also the American Eagle.

Apple Pie

Folks, you don't get more apple pie than I am. Folks, I am apple pie (pi).

If Some People

If some people weren't cursing the darkness, candles would never have been invented.

If Religion

If religion has the total or proven truth, then what is the problem?

Fecal Autointoxication

Students of the world, teachers and professors suffer from fecal autointoxication.

It Is Impossible

It is impossible to kill or abuse another human being, because all that we perceive are characteristics of our own minds, and physical existence is an unproven and an unprovable hypothesis.

To Steal

It is impossible to steal someone else's property, because all that we perceive are characteristics of our own minds, and physical existence is an unproven and an unprovable hypothesis.

To Do Anything

It is impossible to do anything to anyone other than oneself, because all that we perceive are characteristics of our own minds, and physical existence is an unproven and an unprovable hypothesis.

America

America is always on the brink of civil war.

What Is the Alternative?

What is the alternative to the U.S.?

The Only Solution

The only solution to politics is eternal vigilance.

I Would Advise

I would advise black Americans to jump ship, because the Democratic Party is sinking fast.

Pied Piper

Pied Piper means pi(ed) piper. It took me 49 years to figure this one out.

In Quest of

I am in quest of the Holy Grail.

In 1972

In 1972, I am the one who said, "The Fascists are coming," and I am also the one who rang the Liberty Bell. I also drafted the Congress into the military for two weeks of military training. I am also the one that told Congress to tell the media to focus on Angela Davis and Jane Fonda in order to bring the ship of state back on an even keel. I also told Congress to get involved in the antiwar movement. I am also the one that told the Congress to freeze the ranks of all high ranking officers in the U.S. military for the duration of the crisis. I also told Congress to put a black general in charge of the defense of North America, if there was no white general that they could trust. Folks, there is a lot that you do not know about me. I told the Congress to tell the Supreme Court to close the curtains facing the White House and not to open them again until the crisis was over. I challenged President Nixon to a duel, and the Congress was my second. A delegation from the Congress, along with a contingent of American Revolutionary War soldier reenactors, marched over to the White House to retrieve my letter that I sent to the President. The letter was my gauntlet, and Congress went to the White House and retrieved it from the President, and the rest is history.

The Pocket Veto

I am the one who solved the problem of the presidential pocket veto.

The March Towards War

The Democrats in Congress wanted me to slow down the President's march towards war in Iraq, but I told President Bush in an e-mail, "Go, go, go!" At about the same time, my medication failed. I believe some members of the government were trying to silence me.

J. Edgar Hoover

I am the one who told the U.S. military that I wanted only one person killed when I was in the military and that was J. Edgar Hoover.

The Vatican's Records

When I was in the military, I was the one who told the Congress to steal all the Vatican's records, make copies of them, and return the originals to the Vatican.

Nelson Rockefeller

I am the one that told Congress to force Nelson Rockefeller to become Vice President, and then keep him quiet and let him investigate the intelligence agencies of government in a superficial manner, so that Congress can then go in depth into the investigation of the intelligence agencies of government. I told Congress to deny Rockefeller the presidency, if something were to happen to the new President.

Edward Kennedy

Senator Hubert Humphrey asked me if Senator Edward Kennedy should be kicked out of the Senate for his legal problems at the time, and I told him no, but Senator Kennedy should be denied the White House.

The KKK

Senator Hubert Humphrey asked me if the KKK should be made illegal, and I told him no. He also asked me if they should be unmasked, and I said yes. I said they could do whatever they liked so long as they did not break the law.

Hubert Humphrey

Senator Hubert Humphrey offered me his twin daughters, and I refused. I was told not to refuse because Senator Humphrey was very powerful at the time, but I refused anyway. Senator Hubert Humphrey wanted to repay me for making him the most powerful person in the country at the time, because President Nixon was essentially a prisoner in the presidency at the time.

Richard Nixon

In 1972, I am the one who busted President Richard Nixon. After that, he was essentially a prisoner in the presidency until his removal from office.

Preadolescents and Adolescents

Preadolescents and adolescents should be warned that too much masturbation can cause chest pains and that they should do things in moderation. They should be told that they should not masturbate more than two or three times a week, because if they do, they will get chest pains and hair might even start growing on their hands.

If God Is Love

If God is love, then God is also hate, because it is possible to love to hate.

Edward Teller

In 1972, I am the one who told Congress to listen to Edward Teller, because he would be able to understand and explain my ideas to Congress.

William F. Buckley, Jr.

In 1972, I told the Republicans in Congress to listen to William F. Buckley, Jr.

Jesse Jackson

In 1972, I told Congress to tell Jesse Jackson to form an organization within the Democratic Party called The Rainbow Coalition. I also told Congress to tell Jesse Jackson that blacks should stop calling each other niggers, and I also said that, if blacks were to learn how to bluff, there is no limit to how high they can go.

Coretta Scott King

In 1972, I told Congress to tell Coretta Scott King that the struggle should be left up to the courts and that blacks should argue their cases in court. I also said that I thought that Coretta Scott King was sexy.

The Density Effect

The density effect is relative to the density of the medium and the velocity of the fundamental particles that are traveling through the medium. The greater the density of the medium and the greater the velocity of the fundamental particles that are traveling through the medium, the greater the density effect that will be experienced by the fundamental particles that are traveling through the medium.

Political Cartoons

In 1972, I am the one who developed the concept for the "Our Father Was a Liberal" cartoon. I also developed the concept for the U.S.A. as the Frankenstein's Monster cartoon, and I also developed the concept for the cartoon with President Nixon running across the finish line with the horse (representing the U.S.A.) on his back, and I also developed the concept with the ant (representing the poor) under the shoe of the rich saying, "Hi, Rich People, Don't Press Too Hard, Because I Am Alive!" cartoon. I also told Congress that they should protect political cartoonists, because I said that political cartoons are a very powerful medium and that political cartoonists will need protection. I also told government scientists that they should tell cartoonists of all kinds to sell their original cartoons, because people would be eager to buy them.

Muhammad Ali

In 1972, I am the one who told government scientists to tell Muhammad Ali how to beat George Foreman. I told government scientists to tell Muhammad Ali that whenever George Foreman attacked him, he should put his hands in front of his face like a child when a child is being beaten, and George Foreman would not be able to hit him, and if he did not do what I told him to do, George Foreman was going to beat the shit out of him.

Let the Battle Begin

In 1972, I told Congress, "OK, Congress, I think that we probably have everyone now, so it is time to close the doors and let the battle begin in earnest." I also told Congress, "OK, Congress, it is time for miscegenation." And I also told the Congress, "OK, Congress, let the American Experiment begin in earnest."

Fifteen Minutes

All it takes is 15 minutes off the plane and anyone can be American, because what is American about America is what is common to all human beings.

Jewish Termite Mounds

When Jewish termite mounds get disrupted, the Jews say afterwards, "OK, back to work, back to work, back to work!"

Black American Communities

When black American communities get disrupted, the blacks say, "We are not praying hard enough."

White American Communities

When white American communities get disrupted, the white Americans say, "Life is one damn shit after another."

Muslim Communities

When Muslim communities get disrupted, the Muslims say, "Allah is great!"

Chinese Communities

When Chinese communities get disrupted, the Chinese say, "There goes the yin and the yang again."

Indian Communities

When Indian communities get disrupted, the Indians say, "Which god do we pray to this time?"

Japanese Communities

When Japanese communities get disrupted, the Japanese say, "Do we have enough transistors?"

Buddhist Communities

When Buddhist communities get disrupted, the Buddhists say, "We keep forgetting that we are supposed to forget about the world."

Christian Communities

When Christian communities get disrupted, the Christians say, "Christ is surely taking his time."

Jewish Communities

When Jewish communities get disrupted, the Jews say, "Is this in the Bible?"

African Communities

When African communities get disrupted, the Africans say, "Forward to the past."

American Indian Communities

When American Indian communities get disrupted, the American Indians say, "Our ancestors are sleeping on the job again."

West Indian Communities

When West Indian communities get disrupted, the West Indians say, "It is because we can't do anything right."

Russian Communities

When Russian communities get disrupted, the Russians say, "Pour the vodka, and call the Kremlin."

French Communities

When French communities get disrupted, the French say, "We are French, therefore, we should be exempt from stuff like this."

German Communities

When German communities get disrupted, the Germans say, "It is because we are not pure enough."

British Communities

When British communities get disrupted, the British say, "We are British, how dare God do this to us?"

Spanish Communities

When Spanish communities get disrupted, the Spaniards say, "It is because we ran out of gold."

Portuguese Communities

When Portuguese communities get disrupted, the Portuguese say, "It is because we sat on our asses for centuries."

Italian Communities

When Italian communities get disrupted, the Italians say, "It is because we are too close to the Vatican."

Dutch Communities

When Dutch communities get disrupted, the Dutch say, "It is because the world benefited more from our concept of tolerance than we did."

Greek Communities

When Greek communities get disrupted, the Greeks say, "It is because sodomy and Christianity don't mix."

Swiss Communities

When Swiss communities get disrupted, the Swiss say, "Only time will tell."

Latin American Communities

When Latin American communities get disrupted, the Latin Americans say, "It is because we lack and need good dictators."

Scandinavian Communities

When Scandinavian communities get disrupted, the Scandinavians say, "Superior? Superior to what?"

Belgian Communities

When Belgian communities get disrupted, the Belgians say, "It is because nobody knows a damn thing about us."

Eastern European Communities

When Eastern European communities get disrupted, the Eastern Europeans say, "It is because everybody thinks that we are stupid."

Australian Communities

When Australian communities get disrupted, the Australians say, "It is because we are down under."

New Zealand Communities

When New Zealand communities get disrupted, the New Zealanders say, "We are not worried, because the earth's magnetic field is going to flip someday."

Canadian Communities

When Canadian communities get disrupted, the Canadians say, "It is because there is a big gorilla to the south of us."

Turkish Communities

When Turkish communities get disrupted, the Turks say, "It is because our country has the same name as a stupid bird."

Mexican Communities

When Mexican communities get disrupted, the Mexicans say, "Montezuma was more powerful than we thought."

Hawaiian Communities

When Hawaiian communities get disrupted, the Hawaiians say, "It is because luaus have lost their significance for us."

Part Two

Neoliberal Arts

Most people are not aware that by studying neoliberal arts they can become some of the most powerful people in the world. Folks, neoliberal arts is not harmless. If one were to become a good student in neoliberal arts, one can become very powerful, indeed. I chose to be low-keyed, but you do not have to be low-keyed, if you were to become neoliberal artsians.

Now Becoming Apparent

It is now becoming apparent that the slowing of the flow of time inside a medium has more to it than just the density effect, but it also has to do with the nature of the microenvironment of the medium.

The Slowing of Light

The slowing of the velocity of light is always relative to the slowing of the flow of time.

People Who Believe

People who believe that I am opinionated are bigots, because most of my ideas are already history.

Historically Speaking

Historically speaking, personal financial wealth does not mean a damn thing. At best, it is a footnote in history.

The Phallus Symbol

In 1972, I told government scientists that I claim the phallus symbol posthumously, and I told Congress that my sacrament is water, and that they should drink water, because I turn water into come. I also told Congress to masturbate in remembrance of me.

Exploiting Geniuses

Exploiting geniuses for their genius is much better than eating, sacrificing, or ignoring them any day.

Revenge of the Nerds

The nerds are on the rise around the world. Praise the Lord, and Hallelujah!

The Real Intellectual Villains

The real intellectual villains are usually the intellectual insiders, while the real intellectual heroes are usually the intellectual outsiders who are battling the intellectual insiders.

High Energy Electrons

In 1972, I am the one who told the physicists that high energy electrons can be used in high energy particle physics. Before that, physicists believed that high energy electrons could not be used in high energy particle physics, because they would produce gamma rays, but I told them that, at higher and higher energies, high energy electrons would become useful in high energy particle physics research, because the high energy electrons would start producing fundamental particles in particle collisions as the energy of the electrons increased.

Tesla Coil

In 1970, when I was studying electronics at Temple Technical Institute, I created a circuit that produced 20,000 volts from a six-volt battery. My principal told me that I created a Tesla Coil. I used a high voltage capacitor, a high voltage flyback transformer, a diode bridge circuit, and a six-volt battery. The circuit was excited by closing and opening two conductors that were connected to the diode bridge circuit.

Telepathic Circuit

In 1972, I told government scientists about an experiment that I carried out when I was at Temple Technical Institute. I had deliberately short-circuited a power supply diode, and I got the shock of my life, because the *pn* junction communicated with me telepathically, and I had to disconnect the circuit, because the circuit was driving me crazy. I told government scientists to investigate what is going on at the *pn* junctions of power supply diodes when they are short-circuited. I also told government scientists about an experiment that I performed at Temple Technical Institute in which I sent two equal DC currents through the same conductor wire in opposite directions at the same time.

The Fault

The fault for the creation of most of the elitist educational institutions in America lies with the geniuses who made America great, because they are the ones who sponsored or founded most of America's elitist educational institutions. The irony is that most of the geniuses that made America great would not qualify to attend the elitist educational institutions that they sponsored or founded, if they were to return again today as youngsters, which is a sad fact. In other words, they messed up big-time, because smarter is not always smarter.

Gravity

Gravity has to be an instantaneous force, because, otherwise, the gravitational fields of free energy waves would have no meaning, because free energy waves travel at the velocity of light. Therefore, gravity has to be an instantaneous force. Free energy waves have to have gravitational fields, because they have kinetic mass, although they have zero rest mass.

Are Absurd

Free electromagnetic waves are absurd, because electromagnetic waves cannot be exposed and be neutral at the same time.

The Digital Telescope

The idea for the digital telescope started when my principal at Temple Technical Institute, who was a U.S. Navy electronics instructor, told my class that magic eyes were extremely sensitive, and he asked the class if it was possible to make a telescope from magic eyes, and I told him yes. He then asked me how it could be done, and I told him that it could be done by making each magic eye the size of a pixel. He then asked me, "How can it be focused?" And I told him that it could be focused using conventional optics. He said that he will tell the U.S. Navy about the idea, and that is how the digital telescope got its start. The same idea was subsequently used in digital microscopes and digital cameras. The name of the principal was Mr. Miller.

White

If Americans want to be white, then they have to go and fly a kite. In other words, they have to go and perform an experiment.

Into Universal Doubt

I went on my first Cartesian journey into universal doubt when I was about 16 years old, and it made me feel ill for about a month or more.

Two Thousand

In 1972, I told the U.S. military that there might be as many as 2,000 guys like me in the U.S. alone, but I don't think that they are interested in finding them. It is true that guys like me do not like to take orders, but no one in this world is perfect. So what if guys like me question the orders that they are given? So what if guys like me don't give a damn about people in positions of authority? So what if guys like me are always bitching? So what if guys like me are a heap of trouble? :) Don't forget that I saved the damn country, and I did not abuse my position.

I Do Not Recommend

I do not recommend my version of David's slingshot or my version of Benjamin Franklin's kite and key experiment to anyone else, because they are too risky to perform safely.

Madame Tussaud's Wax Museum

In 1975, when I was on vacation in Europe, Richard Nixon followed me to England, and we fought a duel at Madame Tussaud's Wax Museum in London, England, and I ran him through with a sword, and he spent about a month in a hospital in England recovering from his wound. The Congress told Richard Nixon that, if he fought another duel with me, they would have him prosecuted, no matter where in the world he fought the duel with me.

The Captain of the Cricket Team

In elementary and high school, I was the captain of the cricket team. The teachers in charge of sports at my elementary and high school used to call me a classical batsman, and they were both grooming me to become the captain of the Trinidad and Tobago Cricket Team, but I told them that I wanted to go to the U.S.A. to study and live there. I have to admit that I was not a good captain of either cricket team, but both teachers saw potential in me. I was also a spin bowler on both cricket teams. The Trinidad and Tobago government tried to prevent me from leaving the country, but the U.S. Embassy in Trinidad intervened. The Trinidad and Tobago government did not want me to become a scientist, technologist, philosopher, etc., instead, they wanted to keep me in Trinidad and Tobago and make me into a cricketer. The Prime Minister of Trinidad and Tobago at the time, Dr. Eric Williams, told one of the students at my high school to tell me that, if I were to give him the information that I had, he would give me my Ph.D., but I refused to give it to him. The Vatican was also trying to prevent me from leaving Trinidad and Tobago.

Under Surveillance

Since I was a very small child, I was under surveillance by the Vatican, the U.S. government, the Trinidad and Tobago government, and who knows who else.

Niels Bohr

In 1972, I am the one who told government scientists where Niels Bohr buried the bronzed books. Niels Bohr was trying to tell scientists that the education system in the world today is making everyone dumber and dumber. I am also the one who told government scientists to tell Dr. Kildare on the television series on television with the same name to ask, "What is x?" and I told government scientists to tell Dr. Kildare that the answer is poison. Dr. Kildare meant that doctors kill there.

Einstein's Concept of Simultaneity

Einstein's concept of simultaneity is dead as far as I am concerned, because instantaneous communication is a fact in the universe, and gravity is an instantaneous force, and, besides that, teleportation to anywhere in the universe is also possible at faster than the velocity of light.

The Principle of Complementarity

The principle of complementarity in physics is dead as far as I am concerned, because light is a photon wave, and the teleportistic interpretation of quantum mechanics is correct, according to me.

Deadism

Deadism is the philosophical doctrine that states that it is impossible to prove to the dead or for the dead to prove to themselves that they are dead, because if one could prove to the dead that they are dead, then the dead are not really dead, and also, if the dead can prove to themselves that they are dead, then they are not really dead.

The Sensation of Pain

The sensation of pain makes all knowledge seem inadequate, except the knowledge that relieves the sensation of pain.

The Dimensions

The dimensions of an existent object are relative to the velocity of light vectors in a vacuum.

Even Government Scientists

Even government scientists did not want me to succeed academically, because I told them, in 1972, that there is something wrong with the special theory of relativity, and I would try to figure out what it was. That made them angry, because Dr. Jacob Bronowski on the Ascent of Man on public television in the early seventies said that one should not tamper with the special theory of relativity, and I knew that he was speaking to me. He said that one should either accept the special theory of relativity whole, or reject it whole. Scientists were really pissed off at me, and they did all that they could to prevent me from tampering with the special theory of relativity. The VA tampered with my medication when they thought that I was getting close to a solution to the problem that is wrong with the special theory of relativity, because government scientists knew from the beginning that I was capable of finding out what is wrong with the special theory of relativity, and they did all in their power to prevent me from doing so. They did not want me to topple the general theory of relativity also, because they knew that I was capable of doing so. In fact, they thought that I was a menace to dead white scientists, in general, and they were right about that.

If Everyone

If everyone was economically independent of each other, society would collapse, because everyone would tell each other, "Who the fuck needs you?"

At the Present Time

At the present time, the VA is overdosing me, but I feel fine, because I am taking less than the recommended dosage. More power to the Republican Party!

It Is Impossible

It is impossible to destroy the black race without destroying the human race, because all human beings descended from black Africans who lived tens of thousands of years ago.

The Maximum Gravitational Acceleration

The maximum gravitational acceleration in the universe is less than c/s, where c is equal to the velocity of light in a vacuum, and s is equal to one second.

Even If Armageddon

Even if Armageddon were to take place, it would not prove a damn thing, because nothing can prove the truth of any religion, due to the nature of reality. Not even God can prove the truth of any religion, due to the nature of reality.

Not Even God

Not even God can prove that God is God, due to the nature of reality.

I See No Reason Why

I see no reason why God couldn't be a midget. Perhaps, God is a midget.

People Who Say

People who say that they do not care about the future history of humanity probably say to themselves and others that they love humanity.

Someday

Someday, it will be possible to teleport the solar system to anywhere in the universe using advanced technosynergic computers.

To Metamorph Humans

Someday, it will be possible to metamorph humans into anything one might so desire, including frogs, using advanced technosynergic computers.

To Metamorph Anything

Someday, it will be possible to metamorph anything into anything else, including metamorphing frogs into humans, using advanced technosynergic computers.

Its Own Timetable

One cannot rush the struggle between entropy and antientropy, because the struggle between entropy and antientropy has its own timetable.

The Concept of Evil

People who say that it is insane to bring up the concept of evil in this post-modern age are being very ironic, because most of them are evil, and they don't even know it.

Formulas For Explosives

In 1972, I am the one who told government scientists to tell lexicographers to take all the formulas for explosives out of the dictionaries. I also told them to tell the cartographers to take all the sea serpents off the maps of the world. And, I also told Congress to ban the flogging of the asses worldwide.

Three Jokers

In 1972, I told Congress that I was holding three jokers and that I was going to empty the bank, because nothing could beat three jokers. I also told Congress that I was giving them an offer that they could not refuse. I told the military that, if the Congress did not stand up to President Nixon, they should throw the whole Congress in jail, because the Congress was committing dereliction of duty.

Las Vegas

In 1972, I told government scientists to tell Las Vegas that whenever three jokers appear in the same slot machine at the same time, they should empty the casino bank, and give all the money in the casino bank at that time to the person who got the three jokers. Las Vegas asked me how can it be done, since they have to use the money in the casino banks for daily operations, and I told them that they should write a check for the amount in the casino bank at that time. Las Vegas also asked me if they could patent the idea, and I told them yes.

The Real Science Villains

The real science villains are usually the science insiders, while the real science heroes are usually the science outsiders who are battling the science insiders.

Reincarnation

Don't worry folks, because reincarnation will be possible in the future using advanced technosynergic computers.

It Is Possible

It is possible for inertial forces to counteract mutual gravitational forces, therefore, galaxies in space do not necessarily have to fall towards each other, because their inertial forces could counteract their mutual gravitational forces.

Is Violated

The law of the conservation of energy is violated by free energy waves, because free energy waves lose energy over great periods of time, and that is why it is impossible to detect the loss of energy from free energy waves in the laboratory, although free energy waves lose energy over great periods of time. The redshift associated with astronomical objects is due to the violation of the law of the conservation of energy by free energy waves, and it is not due to the so-called "big bang" of creation, which is really crap from a simpletistic perspective.

Correct or Truthful

Instead of striving to be scientific, philosophical, scholarly, literary, esthetically pleasing, journalistic, or religious, one should strive, instead, to be correct or truthful.

A Secret Desire

Whites like their food animals to look white, because whites have a secret desire to eat each other.

Considering the Fact

Considering the fact that the experts were off by a factor of about 50 where the creation of workable television sets were concerned, I might also be off by a factor of about 5, where the creation of advanced technosynergic computers are concerned. In other words, advanced technosynergic computers might be created in as little as 40 years from now.

Mathematics

Mathematics is much more interesting when it is approached from the philosophical perspective than when it is approached from the logical or scientific perspective. When mathematics is approached from the logical or scientific perspective, the damn thing is as boring as hell, but when mathematics is approached from the philosophical perspective, the damn thing is as exciting as ever.

Should Be Taught

Mathematics should be taught from the philosophical perspective, and not from the logical or scientific perspective, because human beings have nervous systems and not microprocessors.

Photon Waves

Free energy waves are photon waves, and not electromagnetic waves, as scientists believe.

Rest Mass

Rest mass consists of standing photon-like waves.

The Reason Why

The reason why I am a disabled veteran is because I was given an overdose of LSD by the U.S. military in my soda, and then I was subsequently interrogated in a psychiatric clinic, but they did not get any information out of me. The reason why I was given the LSD was because I refused to give the three star general in charge of Fort Monmouth the command that he asked me to give him. I did not know what the command was for, so I refused to give it to him, and the general said that he was going to fry my brain with a gram of LSD. I suspected that the command that I was supposed to give was the command to take over the country. I told the general that, if anything were to happen to me that he would be sorry, and that is all the information that he got from me. Officially, my rank was five star general, but I had no intentions of playing the puppet to anyone, because I had my own plans for the country.

Government Psychiatric Abuse

If Americans think that government psychiatric abuse does not occur in psychiatric hospitals across America, then Americans are more naive than even they think. Psychological intimidation and abuse of patients are routine in VA hospitals and other hospitals across America. The VA also experiments on unsuspecting patients at VA hospitals. Folks, the snacks that VA patients get free are laced with experimental drugs. The snacks are handed out to VA patients as if the VA patients were laboratory rats, and that is exactly how medical researchers treat their patients. Folks, the motto of the DAV is, "Still Continuing to Serve" (as laboratory rats?). The DAV has financial assets in excess of $150,000,000.00. Now, where did they get all those assets, and why do they need all those assets?

Even If It Takes

Even if it takes a thousand years, I will still get all my original ideas back from the elitist thieves who have stolen my original ideas over the years, and so will everyone else who have had original ideas stolen from them, because, someday, it will be possible to retrieve the past electronically using advanced technosynergic computers.

No Secure Hiding Place

Someday, death will be no secure hiding place for those who have committed heinous crimes against humanity, because it will be possible to bring those who have committed heinous crimes against humanity back alive again using advanced technosynergic computers and have them tried and executed for every heinous crime that they have committed against humanity.

Six Million Times

Someday, the Jews are going to bring Hitler back alive again using advanced technosynergic computers and execute the son-of-a-bitch six million times.

The Democratic Party

The Democratic Party is sinking fast. More power to the Republican Party!

Wallow in Blackness

Most blacks like to wallow in blackness exclusively.

All High Ranking Officers

I would advise all high ranking officers in the U.S. military not to give any commands, if you do not know what the commands are about, because you could be giving commands to take over the U.S. without knowing it. You should always ask what the commands are about, and, if you are not told what the commands are about, you should refuse to give the commands.

GIs and Disabled Veterans

Folks, GIs and disabled veterans are considered laboratory rats by the Democratic Party and liberals, in general. It is a little known fact that Democrats and liberals, in general, use scare tactics in order to prevent veterans from visiting VA hospitals when they need medical attention. The scare tactics start when the veterans are still in the military and continue after they leave the service.

The Republicans Asked

In about 1973 or 1974, the Republicans in Congress asked me if they should change the name of the Republican Party because of the Watergate Affair, and I told them no. And in 1972, I told them that, if they wanted to save the Republican Party, they should not support President Nixon publicly, but that, if they wanted to support President Nixon, they should do so privately.

A Human Being

A human being cannot be the human body, because all the biologically active atoms that were in one's body a year ago are no longer in one's body today. Therefore, a human being is the human mind, and not the human body. In other words, reincarnation is possible without using the same atoms that the person who is being reincarnated died with. Therefore, true reincarnation will be possible in the future using advanced technosynergic computers.

Labor Unions

Labor unions are good, in theory, but they are disasters in practice.

In This World

In this world, there is a lot to bitch about, and that is what makes the world exciting. If everyone cannot find things to bitch about in this world, then something is seriously wrong with them. Folks, it is good to bitch, because that is what makes the world exciting.

Symphonies

I don't know how symphonies make other people feel, but they make me feel like God.

Does Not Cancel

Negative charge does not cancel positive charge, instead, negative charge neutralizes positive charge.

It Is Not Necessary

It is not necessary to include matter and energy in the probability wave equations, because matter and energy can be considered to be some of the characteristics of the probability waves themselves.

The American Revolution

The American Revolution will probably never be over completely.

Infinitesimals

Infinitesimals are crap, because they are figments of the imaginations of mathematicians, since something cannot be infinitely small and not have zero dimension or dimensions.

Apes Will Be Apes

Apes will be apes, no matter what the context might be.

The Victims of Scare Tactics

The reason why there are so many sick, homeless veterans is because they are scared to visit VA hospitals to seek medical treatment, due to the fact that they were the victims of scare tactics by the Democratic Party and liberals, in general, since they were in the service.

If You the Reader

If you the reader of this aphorism were really the mind of a desktop nonclassical computer, where would the desktop nonclassical computer be located, and who or what is operating the desktop nonclassical computer?

Genes Do Not Converge

Genes do not converge, instead, they diverge. Therefore, all human beings had to originate from black Africans who lived tens of thousands of years ago, because black Africans are the oldest human race.

How Would You the Reader?

How would you the reader of this aphorism go about proving that yesterday was real and not virtual? By virtual, I mean to appear to have been real, but, in fact, was not real.

No Matter How Accurate

No matter how accurate the theory of quantum chromodynamics might be or become in the future, it is still crap, and will always be crap, because gluons are simpletistically absurd.

Scientists

People should enjoy lassoing scientists of all kinds, because most of them are intellectual bovines.

Professional Elites

People should enjoy lassoing professional elites, in general, because most of them are intellectual bovines.

The Big Bangs of Their Orgasms

Scientists are confusing the big bangs of their orgasms with cosmology, because the big bang of creation is crap from a simpletistic perspective.

Jabberwocky

People who believe that the poem, *Jabberwocky*, (from *Through the Looking Glass* by Lewis Carroll) is a great poem are intellectual chimps, because the poem is crap, and it was meant to be crap. In fact, the whole book, *Through the Looking Glass*, is an insult to the intelligence of little girls. Lewis Carroll would never have written a book like that for little boys.

Injustice Anywhere

Injustice anywhere threatens justice everywhere.

The Age of the War of the Computers

The postmodern age is the age of the war of the computers.

A Form of Masturbatory Behavior

War is a form of masturbatory behavior on a grand scale, because all that we perceive are characteristics of our own minds, and physical existence is an unproven and an unprovable hypothesis.

The Ultimate Masturbatory Behavior

The ultimate masturbatory behavior in nature is zero multiplied by or copulating with infinity, while the ultimate masturbatory behavior in the universe is the struggle between entropy and antientropy.

Labor Political Action Committees

Labor Political Action Committees (L-PACs) should replace labor unions, because labor unions are anti-meritocracies when it comes to workers' wages or salaries and benefits.

Sexual Intercourse

Sexual intercourse is a form of masturbatory behavior, because all that we perceive are characteristics of our own minds, and physical existence is an unproven and an unprovable hypothesis.

Solipsism

Solipsism states that all of existence is masturbatory in nature, because all that we perceive are characteristics of our own minds, and physical existence is an unproven and an unprovable hypothesis.

If Most People

If most people as individuals were to work for a thousand years, they still would not equal the contributions that I have made to the U.S. and the world over the years.

It Still Would Not Prove

Even if all the prophecies in the Bible were to be fulfilled, it still would not prove a damn thing, because nothing can prove any religion to be true, due to the nature of reality.

No Evidence

No evidence is sufficient to prove anything with absolute certainty, due to the nature of reality.

Will Make

Advanced technosynergic computers will make all of the life sciences humane.

Are Really Sadists

I would not call most of the scientists in the life sciences scientists, because most of them are really sadists posing as scientists.

Neoliberal Arts and Synergics

Countries that do not adopt neoliberal arts and synergics as academic disciplines are doomed to be left behind, because the future belongs to countries that adopt neoliberal arts and synergics as academic disciplines.

People of Faith

I have nothing against people of faith, but it is just that I like to argue with them. I have been arguing with people of faith all my life, and I will probably do so to the very end of my life. As I grow older, I am beginning to argue with everyone, because, in my youth, I did not realize how flimsy all knowledge really is.

No Country or People

No country or people have any legitimate excuses for not making important contributions to the advancement of knowledge, because there are billions of simple but profound ideas in everyone's environment that no one has discovered as yet.

Life Would Be Boring

If there were no people of faith, life would be boring, because arguing with people of faith is what makes life interesting for me. I like to punch holes in the arguments of people of faith, and besides that, people of faith prevent the world from becoming a scientific nightmare.

Keep Going Back

In 1972, I told Congress that, if they do not keep going back to Benjamin Franklin for inspiration and guidance, they were going to get lost, because the intellectual universe is a very treacherous place, and they have to navigate the intellectual universe very carefully, or else the U.S. ship of state would be doomed to disaster.

Students of the World

Students of the world, as you grow older, you will begin to realize how flimsy all knowledge really is.

Masturbatorism

Masturbatorism is the philosophical doctrine that states that all of nature is masturbatory in behavior, because all that we perceive are characteristics of our own minds, and physical existence is an unproven and an unprovable hypothesis.

Wouldn't Be Safe

If it weren't for people of faith, the streets wouldn't be safe to walk even for scientists, because they will also become the targets of kidnappings by other scientists who are intent on experimenting on them.

Most Poets

Most poets love the poem, *Jabberwocky*, by Lewis Carroll, because it fits very well with their anti-intellectual agenda.

Intellectual Farts

People who believe that the medium is the message are intellectual farts, because the medium is the carrier of the message, and not the message itself.

The U.S. Congress Knew

Since about 1972 or 1973, the U.S. Congress knew all the Vatican's secrets up to then, because I am the one who gave the U.S. Congress the command to steal all the Vatican's records, make copies of them, and return the originals to the Vatican. I also sent the U.S. Congress on many other secret-agent missions in 1972, including the removal of President Richard Nixon from office. I could have become very powerful, but I was not interested in power then or now. My main desire then and now was to liberate geniuses all over the world.

The Cable TV Black Boxes

People who have reason to believe that the U.S. government might have reason to target them for special programming should return their cable TV black boxes to their cable TV companies, because the cable TV black boxes are now computers that the federal or state governments can use to target certain individuals with special programming that can affect them in negative ways. Yes, folks, Big Brother now has access to your private residences through the cable TV black boxes.

Muslim Smart-bomb Technology

The Muslims lead the world in smart-bomb technology, because their smart-bombs are cheap, and they have all the capabilities of human beings. Muslim smart-bombs can even pray to Allah. The West will probably never catch up with Muslim smart-bomb technology, because Muslim smart-bomb technology is constantly improving. Probably the only solution to Muslim smart-bomb technology is the old-fashioned nukes. I believe that the only solution to Muslim smart-bomb technology is the old-fashioned nukes, because Muslim communities seem incapable of and unwilling to stand up to Muslim extremism.

The World

The world must never allow genius to play second fiddle to academic coping skills again.

A Navigator of the Intellect

After studying myself for more than 30 years, I have come to the conclusion that I am a navigator of the intellect, however, I arrived at this conclusion a long time ago.

The Arts and the Humanities

The arts and humanities must stand their ground. The arts and the humanities must yield no ground to the sciences and the social sciences, because, otherwise, the arts and humanities will continue to remain shallow.

Was Enjoying Themselves

From 1972 to about 1976, the U.S. Congress was enjoying themselves, because they were on secret-agent missions that I sent them on in 1972. I even had Congress doing physical exercises everyday in order to keep them in shape. In 1972, I told Congress to see if they could complete the secret-agent missions that I sent them on by 1976, in order to coincide with the 200th anniversary of the American Revolution.

Psychoactive Genes

The way that psychoactive genes are expressed in the human brain has to play a predominant role in human behavior, because, after studying myself for more than 30 years, I have come to the conclusion that I am a prisoner of the way that my psychoactive genes are expressed in my brain.

I See No Good Reason Why

I see no good reason why the universe could not have started at any point in its projected evolutionary history, because the universe might not be fundamental in any sense whatsoever.

Professional Elites

Professional elites are as trustworthy as used-car salesmen, which should make everyone feel really nervous, as it should.

The Neofairness Doctrine

The neofairness doctrine states that creative proficiency should be valued much higher than noncreative proficiency in academia and outside of academia whenever creative proficiency is more useful to the profession, job, or goal that the person is aiming for than noncreative proficiency.

Ever Since

Ever since I was a small child, the U.S. government was scared of me, because they thought that I would take over the world someday. I was surprised that they let me into the country in the first place, because they knew all along that I was trouble. In fact, I think that I appeared in The Little Rascals series on television on more than one occasion when I was a kid. I won't be surprised if the U.S. government told my teachers and professors to make sure that I failed in school and college.

Too Damn Smart

In 1972, a high-ranking sergeant told me that the U.S. government was thinking of blacklisting me or kicking me out of the country, because I was too damn smart. Well, they did not kick me out of the country, so they probably blacklisted me.

Crazy-people Music

Symphonies are crazy-people music, because they make me feel like God.

Index

978-0-595-35857-1
0-595-35857-8

www.ingramcontent.com/pod-product-compliance
Lightning Source LLC
Chambersburg PA
CBHW051428280526
45785CB00003B/1201